Focus on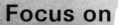

edited by Ray Mit

Our Own Century

Islay Doncaster

Longman

Longman Group Limited
London

Associated companies, branches and
representatives throughout the world.

First published 1971
ISBN 0 582 18236 0

Printed in Great Britain by
E. J. Arnold & Son Limited Leeds

List of Contents

People 1900–1914

At the beginning of the twentieth century people were much more clearly divided into classes than they are today. The upper classes consisted mainly of members of the nobility who got most of their money from the large areas of land that they had inherited. Here you see them in their best clothes at Ascot Races.

The middle classes included some rich factory and mine owners, doctors, lawyers, shopkeepers, clerks and other people who worked with their heads rather than with their hands. Below is a middle class family.

The working classes contained far the largest number of people and consisted of factory workers, miners, dockers, farm workers and many others like them. Some of the lowest paid labourers lived in great poverty, as you can see from the picture of children on the opposite page. It was found that in York in 1899 two people out of every seven did not have enough to eat, nor enough clothes to wear nor enough fuel to keep them warm. Country people, like the labourer on the page opposite, were also paid a very low wage, but they often had a little plot of land on which they could grow a few vegetables.

4

Already at the beginning of the twentieth century some attempts were being made by the government to improve the lives of the less fortunate people. In 1908 laws were passed to give the poorest old people a small pension to live on when they were too old to earn their living. Other laws were passed to pay some money (unemployment benefit) to labourers who were unable to get work through no fault of their own, and to allow certain kinds of labourers to get free doctoring. To pay for this the government had to raise the taxes on the rich. Many people protested, but in the end the government had its way. Lloyd George, the Prime Minister, said, 'This is a war budget. It is for raising money to wage warfare on poverty and squalor'. These laws were the basis of the present system of benefits, but it took another fifty years, as we shall see, before the state was really looking after nearly all the poor people.

Well-to-do homes 1900-14

This picture shows Polesden Lacey, a large country house in Surrey. It stands in a magnificent park and has a beautiful garden, full of flowers, shady walks and fine views. The owners were very rich and used to invite many people down from London for week-end parties. On Sunday morning they went to church in carriages, escorted by footmen. In the afternoon some of their guests went for a drive in the Daimler, wearing special motoring veils to protect them from the dust. Others, putting on their country clothes of thick tweed, went for a walk round the estate. After tea and after dinner, they played bridge (cards).

Below is a picture of a middle class family group of about 1900 who lived less grandly than the owners of Polesden Lacey, but who were still comfortably well-off. What are the differences between their clothes and ours? Look particularly at the collars and footwear of the men, and the dresses and hairstyles of the women.

This picture of a rector and his wife having tea upon the lawn
is typical of many country people who were not so rich as
those who held grand house parties, but who were none
the less quite comfortably off. There were country doctors and
lawyers living in the same kind of way. They probably had a
comfortable house with one or two servants to clean, cook and
serve at table. Outside there was probably a flower garden, and
a kitchen garden and perhaps a shrubbery and an orchard.

The rector and his wife look as if they have a silver teapot
and some elegant china. What do you think they are having for
tea? Perhaps scones, egg
and cucumber sandwiches
and walnut cake.

Below you can see how
many middle class families,
both in the town and in the
country, spent the evenings
at home. There was no
television to watch, no
cinema to go out to, so they
would talk, or perhaps some
one would read or tell a
story.

1900-14 Poor homes in towns

These houses in the East end of London are terraced cottages. Each contains a living room and a separate scullery downstairs, and two bedrooms upstairs. There is cold water in the scullery. At the back there is a yard with an outside lavatory and a line full of washing. There was only one door on to the street, so rubbish had to go out, and coal had to come in, through the living room.

In the lower picture you can see some better working-class houses in Leeds. What advantages can you see?

Are there any houses like these still standing in your home area?

Slum family living room

Here is a picture of the living room of one of the East London terraced houses. They might have had gas lighting but more probably they had to use oil lamps or even candles. There was no bathroom so the family washed in a tub, filled with kettles of boiling water, on the floor. Where did they hang their clothes, and how did they dry their washing? What are the disadvantages of living in a house like this?

Below you can see a picture of children in a street in East London. What differences do you see between their clothes and your clothes?

Country homes 1900-14

This is a picture of a cottage in Warwickshire. In the country at this time most people got their water from a pump or a well instead of from a tap. Which do you think is the more convenient: a pump or a well?

In most labourers' cottages there was a front parlour where the best furniture was kept, and which was used for entertaining visitors, a living room and kitchen combined, an outside scullery and two bedrooms upstairs.

Life in the remote country villages was uneventful: the daily round of agricultural work, church or chapel on Sundays, perhaps a drink at the pub on Saturdays. Any spare time would be spent digging the family vegetable plot. For the women there was an endless round of domestic work such as cooking, washing and cleaning for the family.

The villages were visited by various travelling salesmen. Flora Thompson in her book *Lark Rise to Candleford* describes some of the callers at a tiny Buckinghamshire hamlet at the end of the nineteenth century. From the fruit and fish cart the villagers bought a bloater for their midday meal or an orange or two for the children. From the baker they bought their bread and also, because the baker had once been a ship's carpenter, they heard fine tales of the sea, which most of them had never seen. But farm labourers earned only 12 shillings a week so they could afford very few luxuries.

At the top of village society came the largest landowner. The doctor and the parson might be on good terms with him and his family. Below them came the schoolmaster, shop keepers, the post office clerk, the publican at the inn, the tenant farmers (who rented land from the landowner), and the village craftsmen such as the blacksmith, carpenter, wheelwright, and thatcher. But the vast majority of people in the village at this time were farm labourers employed either directly by the landowner, or by his tenant farmers.

Farmhouses were big rambling buildings surrounded with outhouses, stables, barn, orchard and chicken run. Sometimes the unmarried men employed by the farmer lived with him and his family. They ate their meals in the big kitchen like the one in the picture below. Can you see the kettle hanging over the fireplace ready to make a cup of tea? On the table is a basket packed, perhaps, for a working dinner in the fields. Can you find the bellows hanging on the wall?

If you get the chance to visit a farm try to find out what some of the old buildings were used for fifty years ago. See if you can find the dairy where the milk maids churned the milk into butter and made the cheese. Look for the old copper in the scullery where the water was boiled for the washing, and see if you can find a mangle like the one on the right of the picture. Look for a wall oven: it will be a tunnel behind a door in the wall. A fire was lit in there once a week; when the oven was hot the fire was raked out and the bread and pies for the week were put in to cook.

Work in towns 1900-14

By the beginning of the twentieth century many factories were inspected and the workers in them were not allowed to work more than a certain number of hours. Even so, conditions in the best factories were a long way from those of today. Children were still allowed to work as soon as they were twelve years old. Small workshops were not inspected until 1909 nor were there any laws until then about rates of pay. Such work places were called 'sweat shops' because the employers crammed in as many workers as possible and over-worked and underpaid them. This happened especially in the tailoring trade.

What differences can you see between the two factories shown on this page? Above is a hat factory, below is a cotton mill.

Sixty years ago, many more people earned their living as shop-keepers or by selling goods in the market than do today. What is being sold in this market? Do you know where your nearest market is? Does your market have any stalls like this?

The greengrocer (below) probably ran his own shop alone with occasional help from his family. Look at your local high street and see how many small shops run by their owners you can count. Then count up how many people are employed in the local supermarket or department store. Sixty years ago there were no supermarkets and only in a few large cities were there department stores.

How do Mr. Plumbridge and his shop differ from your local greengrocer?

Work in the country 1900-14
The picture above shows horses drawing a plough to prepare the land for the planting of the seed. How many horses are there? Nowadays the job would be done by a tractor. What are the advantages of a tractor over horses?

The picture below shows the corn harvest. The men are pitchforking the bundles of ripe corn on to the cart. It would then have been stored in a thatched stack or in a barn until the threshing machine came round to separate the corn from the husks and the stalks so that it could be put in bags and sold. This kind of farming used many more men than the combine harvester on page 34.

On downland and hill farms sheep were raised instead of corn. The shepherd trained his dog from six months old by making him work with an older dog. The dog had to learn to guide a flock of sheep. to separate out a few, and many other tasks. Sixty years ago certain sheep in each flock had bells, each of a different note. The tinkling noise was more for the pleasure of the shepherd than to help him find the sheep, according to W. H. Hudson, a writer of that time. Sometimes in the country today, sheep dog trials are held, at which the dogs compete with each other in carrying out the most complicated instructions given by their masters.

The blacksmith was one of the most important men in the village. The farmer depended on him to make and mend ploughs and harrows and to shoe his horses, and the house-wife depended on him to repair her iron fire-tongs, poker and fire-grate. Can you see the fire? What were the bellows used for? Where is the anvil and what was that used for?

When you are next in a country village, see if you can find the workshops of some of these old craftsmen, or go to the local museum to see their tools.

15

Travelling Sixty years ago people going on a long journey had to go by train as there were very few cars. The trains were pulled by steam-locomotives like the *City of Truro* in the picture. It was built in 1903 for the Great Western Railway. You can see it today in the Railway Museum at Clapham. It used to haul the overseas mail special from Exeter to Bristol at an average speed of 70 mph (110 km/h) and was said to have got up to 100 mph (160 km/h) going down a slope. The train was the fastest method of travel for passengers, goods and the mail in those days.

In London people could get to work by underground, but in the early days it was steam-driven and very much more smoky and dirty than it is today. Electrification was only just beginning to provide a cleaner method of travel. Below you can see the Booking Hall at Liverpool Street Underground in 1912. How do the clothes of officials and passengers differ from those of today? The two passengers are city workers.

The newest forms of transport were the motor cars and the motor buses. But cars were still far too expensive except for very rich people, and a bus journey was slow, noisy, and bumpy. What differences do you see between these early cars and buses and the ones we have today?

Steamships had been travelling the oceans for nearly 100 years. Wireless was already being used for warnings. When the *Titanic* (below) sank in 1912 she wirelessed for help. A ship 58 miles (93 km) away picked up the signal and rushed to rescue 700 survivors. How is the *Titanic* different from the *Queen Mary* on page 37?

Amusements

1900-14 Rich people had many sporting amusements. In the winter they went fox-hunting and in the summer they went to the races at Ascot, where there were house parties, and dinner parties and balls every night.

The less well off had other amusements such as the Music Hall, a game of darts at the pub, or perhaps a holiday by the seaside, or an outing with the church or chapel. There were excursions to seaside resorts, and the idea of a family holiday was beginning to catch on. What differences do you notice between the crowd in the picture of Scarborough below and crowds on beaches today?

Things to do Start to make your own book about the twentieth century, and add to it as you read more of this book. It is a good idea to divide the book into chapters either under different dates like this book, or under different topics such as Homes, Schools, War, Transport, and so on.

You might have a section for famous people. Look up the following people in your encyclopaedia for a start: Lloyd George (prime minister), Captain Scott (polar explorer), King Edward VII.

The Science Museum in London has models and actual examples of early cars, bicycles, aeroplanes and agricultural machinery. If you live in London you could go there and draw some of them for your book. If not, you could write to ask the Museum to send you picture post cards and pamphlets about these things.

The Victoria and Albert Museum, London, has examples of costume and furniture of the period, and so have many local museums. Try to find some and draw pictures of them.

Your grandparents may be able to tell you where they first went to work, how many hours they worked each day and what their pay was. Perhaps they can also describe the kind of house they lived in and any journeys they went on. You could write down what they say. If you have a tape-recorder, record what they say.

Your local library and museum probably have pictures of your town or village as it was 60 years ago. Try to find out how many of the buildings in those pictures are still standing. When you know the names of some of them, then you can get hold of a street map and colour these buildings in. Put a key to the map to say what the colour means, and then add it to your book.

If you and your friends can find out enough about early cars and buses, and costume in this period, you could make a street scene. You could make a background of houses, and then either stick on pictures of vehicles and people, or make little models of them.

War on land 1914-18

In August 1914 Britain went to war against Germany in order to help France. The Germans advanced through France, so an army of volunteers from Britain and the Empire was landed there to try to stop them. The Germans halted at the River Marne and both armies dug themselves into long lines of trenches. Here they remained for three years with a 'no man's land' of barbed wire entanglements between them. Each side tried in vain to shift the other by bombardments followed by raids of foot soldiers. Life in the trenches was very hard. Men were kept there for ten days at a stretch and then given a week behind the lines in which to recover. This is a poster to recruit more people for the war effort. It was designed by Baden Powell. Can you find out more about him?

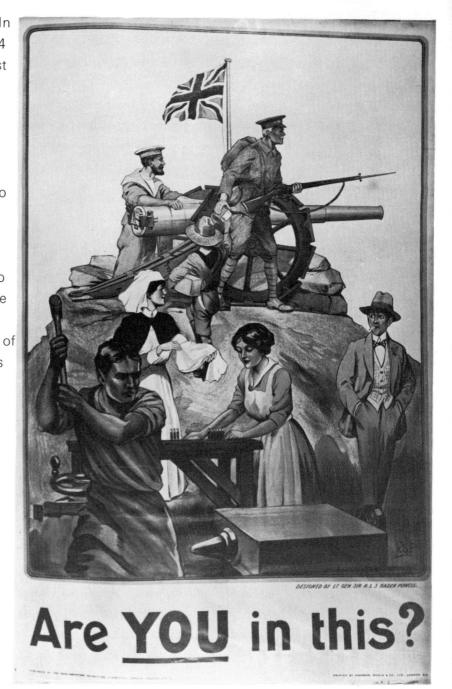

DESIGNED BY LT GEN SIR R S S BADEN POWELL.

Are YOU in this?

So many of the volunteers were killed that in 1916 conscription had to be introduced. By conscription, men between certain ages were forced by law to join the army. In 1915 gas was used as a weapon, first by the Germans and then by the British. But when it was found that the wind could sometimes blow it back in the faces of friends instead of over to the enemy it was not used any more.

The tank was invented by the British and first used successfully in November 1917. Look at the picture on the left and decide what are the great advantages of the tank. Compare this tank with the armoured car on page 43.

Although motor vehicles were coming into use during the war, horses still played a much larger part. They were used to pull wagon-loads of ammunition and food for the troops and also for hauling guns into position. Often they had to drag their heavy loads through thick mud as you can see from the picture above. Can you see what has happened to one of the horses? Later, conditions were so bad that mules were used instead of horses. Draw a picture of a horse at work in the war.

War at sea 1914-18
Battleships like H.M.S. *Indefatigable* (above) were the main fighting force.

One of the most important weapons of the war at sea was the torpedo, fired from submarines like the German one in the picture below. In May 1915 a submarine sank the British liner *Lusitania* and over 1,000 people were drowned. In 1917 the German submarines were ordered to sink at sight all ships in the war zone. It was only the organisation of a British system of convoys of naval ships for all merchant ships that protected British shipping, which was bringing food and military supplies to this country.

War in the air

The Germans used airships, or Zeppelins, for spotting the movements of ships at sea and for bombing. In June 1917 in one raid on London there were 580 dead and wounded.

Aeroplanes were developed by both sides during the war. Fighters, like the one in the picture, were equipped with machine guns. Other planes were used as bombers.

People at home in Britain suffered from food shortages because German submarines prevented merchant ships from bringing food to Britain from abroad. Shortage meant high prices and long queues for meat, butter, margarine and fish. In 1917 the government had to fix prices, and in 1918 certain foods had to be rationed.

The First World War finally ended with the defeat of Germany in 1918. The cease fire was at 11 a.m. on November 11th. Britain had lost 750,000 men. Germany and France each lost a million and a half men.

People in the 1920s and 1930s

The war had forced people of all kinds to fight together, and to endure food shortages and air raids together, so after the war there were fewer differences between classes.

Clothes made out of new man-made materials, such as rayon, were cheaper and it became more difficult to see from a person's clothes what class he or she belonged to. On this page you can see the fashions of the well-to-do people in the early 1920s. Notice that the women's skirts are shorter than before the war.

Immediately after the war people wanted to get better conditions for themselves. Most men now worked only 48 hours a week instead of the 60 or 72 hours of before the war. But unfortunately many workers found that their lives were worse rather than better, because they could not find a home or a job. The people in the picture below look rather unhappy. What are the main differences between them and those in the pictures above?

The war affected the position of women. Many of them had worked in factories making weapons and ammunition, others had worked in the new women's services, so they did not want to go back to being tied to the home. From this time onwards there were many more women out at work. Women also got the right to vote for members of Parliament, which was something that previously only men had been able to do. Women celebrated their new independence by wearing short dresses, and smoking, and going out alone. But though they tried in many ways to show that they were as good as men, they also tried to increase their feminine charms by wearing make-up on their faces — something which until this time had only been done by actresses.

On this page you can see some of the fashions of those women of the late 1920s. Compare them with women's clothes before the war.

Homes in towns 1918-38

Many houses like this were built in the period between the wars to provide homes for the increasing number of middle class people. They usually contained a separate drawing room and dining room, kitchen, bathroom, cloakroom, and outside a garage and a garden. The housewife probably did most of the work herself, with just a cleaner, because since the war there were fewer living-in servants. But she could now order food on the telephone and have it delivered. Houses of this kind were built on the edge of large towns, away from the overcrowded centres. These districts are called suburbs and are really neither town nor country. Long lines of trams, and later trolley buses and buses, had to be built so that suburb dwellers could get to their work.

In your area look round to see if you can find examples of the different kinds of houses shown on this and the next page. Then on a local street map, colour in where they are to be found. Use a different colour for each kind of housing and put a key to the colours at the bottom of the map, so that other people can understand it. Which kind of houses are farthest from the centre?

At the bottom of page 26 you can see working class houses of
Birmingham in the 1930s. How do they differ from those of before 1914
on page 8? Though the government had passed Acts of Parliament and
had given grants of money to local councils to persuade them to build
new houses for the working people, not many of them had been able to
do so. George Orwell, in *The Road to Wigan Pier*, writes, 'As you walk
through the industrial towns, you lose yourself in a labyrinth of little
brick houses, blackened by smoke, festering in planless chaos round miry
alleys and little cindered yards where there are stinking dustbins and
lines of grimy washing, and half ruinous w.c.s'. He points out that not
even the miners, who came home coal-black from the pits, had hot
water laid on, let alone proper bathrooms.

Some town councils did begin to put up new housing estates for
workers. Above is a picture of Quarry Hill council flats site, Leeds, as it
was in 1938. The flats are all planned to face the sun, and the scheme
included communal laundries for the tenants, and parks and playgrounds.
Birmingham and other large cities have also done a great deal to rehouse
their workers.

What do you think would be the main differences between living in a
back to back house and in one of these flats?

Strike 1926 After the war there were many men out of work or working for low wages, particularly in the coal industry, which was declining in importance. The miners tried to get better conditions by striking or refusing to work. In 1926 the miners were supported by most other working men and there was a General Strike which threatened to bring the whole country to a standstill. It lasted for nine days. With all the transport workers on strike the government had to organise volunteer drivers of buses, trains and lorries in order to get people to work, and food and essential supplies to the places where they were needed. The call for volunteers was answered by what was nicknamed the 'plus-four brigade'. These were the young middle class men from universities who wore baggy tweed breeches for their country weekends. These, and other young men, drove buses, handled milk lorries and even drove trains; middle class ladies ran canteens for them.

How do you know the people in these pictures are volunteers, not ordinary workers? Can you think why they had to wire up the bus, and why there is a soldier on duty?

Unemployment in the 1930s

Even so, in spite of the strike, the position did not improve. This was not anybody's fault but was due to the fact that prices for coal, iron and steel fell all over the world. Therefore wages could not go up and more men were turned away from work. Because trade was so bad the government decided to economise: one of the methods chosen was to cut down the unemployment benefits. The amount paid to an unemployed man now depended on what other members of the family were earning. In protest against this many workers' unions organised hunger marches. Above is a picture of the shipbuilders marching to London from Tyneside, where the ship-building yards had been closed down. Because there was no way of improving trade in these heavy industries, nothing much could be done for them.

During the 1930s some men remained unemployed for years. In a book called *Love on the Dole* written at this time, Walter Greenwood tells how it was scarcely possible to get married or to live a normal family life if you were unemployed because the unemployment benefit was so low. In this picture you can see men queueing for the 'dole' which was all they and their families had to live on for weeks at a time.

New opportunities for work 1918-38

Though older industries such as coalmining and shipbuilding were declining, there were other new industries developing to provide opportunities for work. The motor car industry was booming. New methods of work produced more cars more quickly. Each man specialised in one stage of the work only. What are the men in the picture above specialising on? Below you can see wheels being carried by conveyor belt.

This system was called mass production. In 1924 100 men could produce 73 cars in a year; by 1936 they could produce 147 cars. Do you know how many cars are produced by 100 men in one of today's factories?

The electrical goods industry was another that was expanding and providing work for many people. As you can see from the picture above, the conditions in this and other new light industries were cleaner and more modern than in heavy industry. Hours of work were getting shorter, and holidays with pay were gradually being introduced.

Below is a picture of bank clerks at work. In the 1920s and 1930s this was a very secure job with good prospects of promotion and pay. Opportunities in clerical work were increasing all the time: government offices and private firms needed armies of clerical workers, many of them women.

Living in the country 1918-38

In some parts of the countryside village life was decaying. In farming areas machines took over so much of the work that there were fewer jobs. Therefore young people left the villages to work in towns. Old cottages like these in the picture were condemned to be pulled down by the local authorities because the owners could not afford to instal proper sanitation. If the villages were prosperous, perhaps because there was a quarry, a brickworks or railway where the men could get work, the inhabitants might be rehoused. Otherwise the families moved right away.

What do you think was lacking in these houses that most people have today? What were the disadvantages of living in them?

In other parts of the country villages became prosperous. As travel became easier with the development of cars and buses, middle class people began to buy old country cottages. They repaired them and put in bathrooms and laid on water and electricity and used them for weekends and holidays. In the picture above you can see how well the houses and gardens have been looked after. It became very fashionable to have a cottage in the country and in some villages, especially those near the big towns, 'weekenders' and holiday makers from the towns began to take the place of the farm labourers.

As working hours became shorter, and holidays with pay more frequent, working people also began to explore the countryside, either by bicycle or in a coach. How do the clothes and the bicycles of the cyclists compare with today's?

Work in the country 1918-38

In some parts of the country you could still see horses ploughing, reaping, sowing and carting in the 1920s and the 1930s, but the horse was gradually being replaced by the tractor. The tractor is quicker, it can pull a heavier load and it needs less looking after than the horse. In the first picture below you can see horses pulling a reaping and binding machine. It cuts the corn and ties it in bundles. Two men then have to pick up the bundles and put them in stucks to dry. Then the bundles have to be carted and stacked until the threshing machine comes round to thresh out the grains of corn. The other picture, taken after the Second World War when these machines became more common, shows a combine harvester at work. The combine both cuts and threshes the corn. What are the advantages of the combine?

If you get a chance to visit a farm, try to find out how long it takes to plough or to harvest a field, first with horses and then with tractors. It will probably be only the older men who can tell you about the horses.

Village craftsmen

As the twentieth century continues the village craftsmen play a less and less important part in village life. Some blacksmiths have turned themselves into engineers who can mend tractors and other agricultural machinery, but many more have disappeared. Wheelwrights disappeared with the horses, and carpenters and coopers became unnecessary as more and more articles could be bought ready-made.

Some craftsmen have adapted themselves to changing conditions. What sort of baskets is the basket-maker producing? The thatcher no longer has corn ricks to thatch, but there are still thatched cottages. Can you see how the thatch is held down?

When you are in the country it is always worth visiting the museum in a village or a market town. There you will probably find the tools and the products of these old craftsmen, as well as the old horse-drawn ploughs, and the hand tools used for threshing, hedging, sheep shearing, butter and cheese making. Draw pictures of whatever you find, and be sure to write underneath their names and what they were used for. The biggest museums for country things are The Museum of English Rural Life in Reading, Shibden Hall in Halifax, and The Agricultural Gallery of the Science Museum in London, but there are also many small and interesting local museums all over the country.

Travel 1918-38

By the 1920s it was possible for ordinary middle class people to own a car. Many families bought an Austin 7 like the one in the picture above. It cost £165 in 1924. How does it differ from a modern Mini?

Buses with roofs were produced so that people no longer had to wear special thick clothes for a coach journey. Gradually the roads began to fill with traffic and to become increasingly dangerous. In the 1930s pedestrian crossings and the 30 mile-an-hour speed limit in towns were introduced to try to make the roads safer.

For the mass of working class people who could not afford cars, there were increased opportunities for travel by train. Now that many workers had paid holidays they could take their families away to the seaside. Factories sometimes organised day excursions for their workers on bank holiday. The people in the picture below are going, in 1927, on a 'Land Cruise' round the beauty spots of part of Western England.

The *Queen Mary* was built on Clydebank (Scotland) and launched in
1934. She sailed between Southampton and New York with 2,139
passengers and 1,101 crew aboard, the biggest liner then afloat.
In 1936 she made a record crossing of the Atlantic in 3 days, 23 hours
and 57 minutes.

The most spectacular new form of travel was the aeroplane. After
the first direct crossing of the Atlantic had been achieved, passenger-
carrying airlines were gradually developed to take people all over
the world. The Douglas DC/3 in the picture below carried 28—36
passengers at 175 mph (280 km/h). How does that compare
with the speed and size of a modern jet airliner?

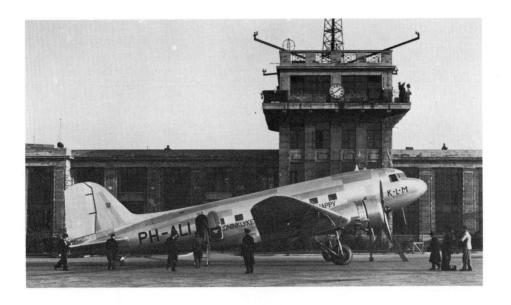

Amusements 1918-38

The wireless was
one of the great new
entertainments of the 1920s.
For the first time people
could hear music, plays,
sport and the news broadcast
in their own homes. Here
is a picture of one of the
earliest of the B.B.C.'s
recording studios.

For an evening out, there was the cinema,
First of all films were silent: you can see
a picture of Charlie Chaplin, the pathetic
but comic little man in baggy trousers who
made everyone laugh at the silent screen.
In the 1930s sound films developed.
There were all kinds of films: cartoons,
Westerns, gangsters, and funny men like
the American Marx Brothers you can see in
the picture below. Some of these old
films are shown on television today and
you can learn quite a lot about people
of the inter-war years by watching them.

Here you can see the crowds at the seaside. What difference do you notice between these crowds and today's crowds? Blackpool, Margate and Southend were developed to provide holiday amusements for all the workers who now had holidays with pay. In 1935 the first Butlin's Holiday Camp was opened at Skegness.

The great weekly excitements during the 1930s in the towns were greyhound racing and soccer. Football supporters watched the progress of their club with enthusiasm and got as excited then as they do now if the team reached Wembley. Below you see the West Ham supporters at Wembley in 1923. Are they very different from today's supporters? Football pools began in the 1930s and reached, through the newspapers and the post, an even wider circle of people than those who could come to the matches.

Education 1918-38

Below is a picture of an elementary school class in 1925. What differences are there between that classroom and your classroom today? After the First World War children had to continue their education until they were fourteen, instead of twelve, and they were no longer allowed to work except as newspaper boys. There were some state secondary schools and some free places in fee-paying schools for clever children, but there were not nearly enough. Most children stayed in the same school until they left at fourteen. Children were medically examined in school and some help was given to parents to pay for treatment. In some parts of the country cheap school meals were provided, but not everywhere as they are today.

Children whose parents could afford it, were sent to private fee-paying schools — as some still are today. Boys usually started at a preparatory boarding school at about eight years old, then they went on to another boarding school at thirteen. Some of these boarding schools, such as Eton, Harrow, Winchester are very old, and very famous.

Things to do Collect some more
material for your book on the twentieth
century. Remember that as well as books
and pictures in school, the most
important sources of information are
museums, libraries and people themselves.
Your own relations and the older people
you meet on holiday will be able to tell
you a great deal. There are suggestions for
the kind of things to look for and to
ask on pages 19, 26, 34, 35.
Here are some names of famous people to
look up in your encyclopaedia:

    King George V and Queen Mary
    Stanley Baldwin (Conservative
    Prime Minister)
    Ramsay MacDonald (Labour
    Prime Minister)
    Amy Johnson (Solo woman air pilot)
    Charlie Chaplin (film star)
    Greta Garbo (film star)
    Malcolm Campbell (speedboat and
    car racing)
    Donald Bradman (cricketer)

Try to collect as much information as you
can about the General Strike of 1926.
You will discover the names of some of the
strikers' leaders and what exactly they
were demanding, and you will have to
find out just what the problems of the
government were. Then you and a group
of friends could write a short news sheet.
It could contain articles describing events,
appeals for volunteers, accounts of the
difficulties of the strikers, and so on. There
is a book called *The General Strike*, 1926,
in the *Then and There* Series published
by Longman which would help you.

War 1939-45

When Hitler, the Leader of Nazi Germany, invaded Poland, Britain and France declared war on Germany (September 3rd 1939). A British army was sent to France, but in 1940 the German tanks, coming right through Holland and Belgium, invaded France and drove the British army into the sea at Dunkirk (see above). Most of the British equipment was lost, but the men were saved because masses of British ships answered the call for help by sailing across the Channel to the rescue. These were not naval boats but all kinds of private and pleasure boats which gallantly came to do what they could.

People of certain age groups were called to fight and only those in essential war work at home or those with very strong principles against fighting could refuse. Which of the services do these men and women belong to?

At first the British Commonwealth was alone against the Nazis, fighting on the sea and in the air, but in June 1941 the Russians joined the British. In December the Americans, after they were attacked by the Japanese, also joined the British.

War on land

Fighting on land was very different from the fighting in the First World War. Instead of soldiers remaining in trenches holding the battle line for months, they were on the move in tanks and armoured cars. Here you can see the armoured cars which drove the Germans out of the North African desert. Compare them with the tanks used in the First World War. What are the advantages of the armoured cars?

In the picture below you can see the British and Americans landing in France in 1944. From there they went on to invade Germany, and, with the help of the Russians advancing from the other side, to win the war against Germany.

War in the air

In 1940, when Britain still had no allies, Germany tried to destroy the Royal Air Force in daylight raids, and when that failed, the German air force carried out night bombing raids on London and other big cities. It was Spitfires and Hurricane fighter planes that kept the Germans at bay in this Battle of Britain. If they had not been able to do so, Hitler would probably have invaded Britain as he had invaded so many other countries. How does the Spitfire compare with earlier planes? It could travel at between 300 and 350 mph (480 and 560 km/h). Notice the machine guns, 4 in each wing.

British scientists developed a system of radar by which enemy aircraft could be spotted on a screen long before they could be seen with the naked eye. This meant that British planes had warning so that they could get up quickly to meet the Germans in the air.

Near the end of the war the German scientists invented the flying bomb. It was an automatic aeroplane, fired by a catapult. It dived and then exploded on landing. In 1944 they produced rocket bombs. They travelled faster than sound, which meant that Londoners heard the bomb exploding before they heard the rocket approaching.

War at sea

The war at sea was important to Britain because she had to get essential food and supplies from abroad. Merchant ships had to be protected from German submarines (above) by convoys. Later in the war the development of radar was a great help in spotting enemy submarines.

The biggest naval battle of the war was in May 1941. The heavily armoured German battleship *Bismarck* (below) came out into the Atlantic. She damaged one British battleship and sank a battle cruiser, and then broke away from the British ships attempting to close in on her. It was the aircraft from the aircraft carrier *Ark Royal* (bottom) which found her and damaged her with their torpedoes. Finally the British battleships were able to finish her off. Later the *Ark Royal* herself was sunk by German submarines.

War at home

The Second World War involved people at home more than the First World War. Clothes, food and petrol were rationed and the price of necessities was controlled. This prevented rich or powerful people from getting more than anyone else of the little that was available. Everyone had a ration book, and was allowed to use only so many coupons per week. Therefore whatever was in short supply, because the merchant ships could not get through, was shared fairly.

Women played their part in the war, not only in the women's fighting services, but also at home where they took the place of men who had gone to fight overseas. What are women being asked to do in the poster on the right?

Below you can see a family going into the air raid shelter in their garden, when the siren has sounded to say that enemy bombers have been sighted. They are carrying gas masks in their boxes.

NATIONAL SERVICE W/33

10,000 Women Wanted For Farm Work

A FREE OUTFIT, high boots, breeches, overall and hat.

MAINTENANCE during training.

TRAVELLING expenses in connection with the work.

WAGES 18/- per week, or the district rate, whichever is the higher.

MAINTENANCE during terms of unemployment up to four weeks.

HOUSING personally inspected and approved by the Women's War Agricultural Committee in each County.

WORK on carefully selected farms.

PROMOTION, good work rewarded by promotion and higher pay.

AFTER THE WAR, special facilities for settlement at home or overseas.

DON'T DELAY ENROL TO-DAY

Application Forms may be had at all Post Offices & Employment Exchanges.

DIRECTOR GENERAL OF NATIONAL SERVICE.
ST. ERMINS, S.W. 1.

German bombs were dropped on big cities as well as on military targets and they did a lot of damage. Here is a picture of a bomb crater in London. Many people were killed or injured in these air raids and thousands lost their homes and possessions.

Below you can see children being evacuated — that is, sent to the country to be out of the way of the bombs. Why have the children got labels? What was in the boxes?

You can probably find out more about the Second World War by asking your parents, grandparents and uncles and aunts, than by any other method. Ask them to tell you what they remember of rationing, air raids, evacuation. See if you can find anyone who was at Dunkirk, El Alamein, or D-Day and ask them to describe it to you. See if you can find anyone to tell you about the Battle of Britain, or the war at sea. Write down what they tell you in your book.

People 1945-70

The Second World War ended in 1945 after the Germans had been defeated in Europe and the Japanese had been defeated in the Far East. Because all classes of people had fought side by side against the enemy both at home and abroad, many of the differences between classes that we mentioned earlier on in the twentieth century, had by now been smoothed away. Also, as we shall see later, a great effort had been made to get rid of the poverty, unemployment and poor housing of pre-war days.

After the shortages and the rationing of the war years, clothes and fashions became long and full as you can see from the picture of the 'New Look', above. Clothes became cheaper and more varied especially with the increase of nylon and other man-made fibres. In the 1950s life became increasingly comfortable for larger numbers of people. More television sets, washing machines, refrigerators, and cars were bought than ever before. This was made possible by the extension of hire purchase; people were, and are, able to use their furniture or fridge while still paying for it in instalments.

What do you notice about the differences in clothes between the 1940s (above) and the 1960s (below)?

Teenagers have attracted more attention since the 1950s than they ever did before the war. They are much better paid, and are therefore more independent of their parents. Many more young people marry under the age of 21 and live away from their parents. They make their own amusements. How are these different from those of their mothers and fathers?

What are the differences in teenage fashions from the 1950s to the present day? Much more attention is paid to men's fashion now than before the war. A tremendous range of clothes is now available to teenagers. In the past they wore copies of grown-up clothes, but now they wear clothes specially designed for them.

Rebuilding the towns 1945-70

In some big cities which had been badly bombed during the war, emergency houses had to be put up quickly to provide homes for those who had been bombed out. Here you can see some of these houses. They were called prefabricated houses because they were made up in factories. They were quickly assembled, but what do you think were the disadvantages of living in them? Later on more permanent houses and flats were put up, but there were still some 'prefabs'.

In your town can you tell the difference between houses built before the war and those put up after the war? On a map of your area colour in with different colours the old houses and the new houses and flats built since 1945.

Since the war new towns have been built to which people from the
overcrowded old towns can be moved. They were planned to be
more attractive and healthier places to live in. The factories were
separated from the houses so that people at home should not be
troubled by noise and smell. New shopping centres were built
like the one at Stevenage (above). What are the differences
between this centre and a High Street in an old town? Why is
family shopping more convenient here?

New towns have neighbourhood centres so that for everyday
needs the family can shop within walking distance. In Stevenage
each neighbourhood has a pub, a selection of food shops, a
primary school, and a chapel and hall. In the picture below notice
the convenient car park and bicycle stands.

Work 1945-70

Working conditions have improved since the war. Hours are shorter (the average in 1965 was 44 hours a week), pay is higher but so are prices, of course, and places of work are pleasanter. The coal and railway industries have been nationalised. This means that they are now run by the state instead of by private owners. Here is a picture of pit-head baths for miners. Below you can see a picture of modern factory conditions. Try to find out from people who work in your local factories what facilities they provide; ask about sport, for instance. Then ask any retired factory workers what conditions were like in their day. It is particularly worth asking first young people, and then retired people, how many hours of work they do or did a week.

One of the reasons why working hours are shorter is because there are now more machines to do the work. On the land the combine harvester and the electric milker have reduced manual labour. Why do you think more eggs are produced by these hens living in a 'battery' than by hens running about in the farmyard?

In factories more and more of the work can be done automatically by machine instead of by men. In the picture on the left the man pressing the buttons can operate an automatic system of storage of pressings of car bodies. The machine automatically pigeonholes the pressings and can find them again in a few minutes. In the past they had to be wheeled by truck.

Education 1945-70

In 1944 an Education Act was passed which changed the education system. Perhaps the most important thing it did was to arrange for every child to go to a secondary school and for all state secondary schools to be free. Some secondary schools were called Grammar Schools and others Modern Schools. In many areas these schools are now being combined into Comprehensive Schools. This is a London Comprehensive School taking most of the pupils from the neighbourhood. London was one of the first areas to build comprehensive schools after the war.

How old do children have to be now before they can leave school? Some stay longer than this age in order to get a better education and therefore a better job. Can you find out from your parents or grandparents how long they had to stay at school and what subjects they studied?

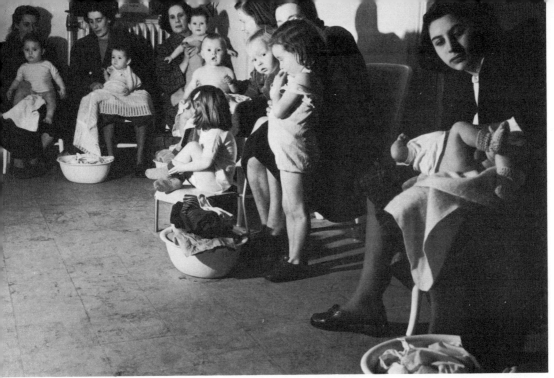

Welfare

Welfare In 1946 the National Insurance Act and the National Health Act established the Welfare State. This means that in return for the workers' contribution towards their weekly insurance stamps, the state, for the first time, provides help for the whole family all through their lives. Above you can see the baby clinic where a mother can get free treatment for her baby. She can also get free doctoring for herself and the rest of her family. If a worker is ill or out of a job, he or she can get sick pay or unemployment pay. Women at the age of 60 and men at the age of 65 are given an old age pension (below).

Amusements 1945-70

Since the war hours of work have got shorter and wages in many kinds of work have gone up. Therefore more people have more free time. This has meant a great expansion in entertainments, particularly in what are called mass entertainments. From the wireless and television, people can get entertainment for longer hours and in more variety than ever before. If you look at the television programmes of one channel as they are set out in the *Radio Times* or the *TV Times*, and make lists of the hours devoted to each of the following topics, you will get some idea of the variety: serious music, light music, panel games, news, sport, plays, serious features, children's programmes, educational

programmes. The result is that many families stay at home and watch the television instead of going out to the cinema as they would have done before the war.

Sport continues to attract many people in their spare time, particularly through television, and through betting on the football pools.

Many teenagers like to go outside home for their entertainment. These are teenagers of 1960. What are they doing?

Never before have so many people been able to go on holiday. Many more people go abroad than did before the war, and quite a number take cars and caravans. The picture above was taken in 1957. How can you tell it was not taken in a camping site today? What has made it possible for so many people to go on holiday, and why was it not possible earlier?

Most people still go in search of the sun and the sea, but some now have a more serious purpose; they go to study buildings, or art or to learn a foreign language. The people on the left are visiting Hampton Court in Middlesex.

Holiday travel has been made much easier and cheaper by the development of what is called the package trip. This means that a group of people all wanting to go to the same place at the same time let a travel agent arrange everything for them. This makes everything much cheaper for everybody.

New forms of travel 1945-70

The most spectacular new forms of travel are in the air. The jet engine, invented towards the end of the war, has made it possible to go faster, to carry heavier loads, and to go further without refuelling. The Comet (above), by the 1950s could cruise 10 miles (13 km) up in the sky at a speed of 12 miles (18 km) a minute. It carried 80 passengers. In 1952 a Canberra made the first double crossing of the Atlantic Ocean in one day. In 1970 the jumbo jet (below) was first used to cross the Atlantic. It carries 345 passengers. It only takes 7 hours to fly from London to New York. Look up Alcock and Brown in your encyclopaedia and find out how long it took them on the very first flight across the Atlantic in 1919.

For short trips between cities, the helicopter has been developed. It can take off and land in a much smaller space than an aeroplane. Why is this an advantage?

The most exciting invention in travel by water is the hovercraft. It goes faster than ordinary ships because it travels on a cushion of air which prevents it being slowed down by the friction of the water. This hovercraft crosses the Channel in 35 minutes. It can carry 250 passengers and 32 cars.

On the railways the great change has been from steam to electric and diesel engines. They make travelling by train much cleaner than before. Everything in the train below is automatic. There is a driver to make sure nothing goes wrong, but there is no guard and even the tickets are checked by machine.

Exploration of space
The most spectacular achievement
of the 1960s was the exploration of space. Rockets are very expensive and
therefore have been developed mainly by Russia and the United States
of America which are large, rich countries. First of all the Russians and
Americans launched unmanned spacecraft. Then they sent up spacecraft
with animals, such as dogs, and eventually the Russians sent up one with
a man in it. It was the Americans who first landed men on the moon on
July 21st, 1969 in the lunar module Apollo 11. Here you can see
Neil Armstrong placing the American flag on the moon.

Artificial satellites help us in all kinds of ways. For instance,
Telstar relays radio and television, and Echo satellites relay telephone
conversations, music and pictures all over the world. Tiros satellites,
revolving round the earth at 450 mph (720 km/h) have taken pictures
of the development and movement of tropical storms.

Things to do You will be able to add some more pictures and notes to your book on the twentieth century.

Here are some useful sources of information:

1. Old copies of illustrated magazines such as *The Illustrated London News, Picture Post, Country Life*. You can find these in the Public Library.

2. Museums and Libraries: The Science Museum in London will provide you with the latest scientific discoveries. Your local museum and your public library should be able to help you to find out about local industry and agriculture, and local modern buildings.

3. People: These are the kind of questions to ask members of your family, and any grown-ups you may meet who live in places different from your home. For instance, if you live in a town, try to find someone who lives, or has lived, in the country. Try to find out what their schools were like, and what hours of work and working conditions were like when they first started to work. Get them to tell you what changes in houses, furniture and clothes they have seen in the last twenty years. Ask them about their amusements when they were teenagers. They will probably be able to tell you what buildings have gone up in the last twenty years, and what changes there have been in travel.

Here are some suggestions for maps to add to your book.

1. On a street map of your area colour in all the buildings put up in the last twenty years.

2. On a map of your county put in the main transport routes.

When you have finished your book, put a list of contents at the front, and make an index for it. Then perhaps you could make a cover for it with a picture which sums up the twentieth century for you.

Get together a group of friends and between you collect as much information as you can from museums, encyclopaedias, and old newspapers about the first flight in space in 1960. Then try to write either a news sheet of reports and 'features' or a radio or television script for an interview with Neil Armstrong.

Now that you know a good deal about all the many changes that have taken place during the twentieth century, write a story about a person or about a family that has lived through them. If you have any grandparents they might help you to write their life story, or the life story of their parents. Or you might make it an imaginary story.

Main landmarks in people's welfare

1906   Compensation to workers for injuries was extended to cover most occupations.

1909   First pensions paid to people too old to work.

1909   Inspection and minimum wage laws extended to sweated industries.

1911   National Insurance began in certain trades. Workers contributed each week to buy a stamp and then were given payments of money when they were unemployed.

1920   Unemployment payments were extended to cover most trades.

1925   Pensions to be paid to widows and orphans as well as to old people. Working people to contribute to buying stamps to help pay for this.

1931   Unemployment payments made subject to a Means Test. This meant that the unemployed man got less if other members of the family were earning.

1945   Family allowances. This meant that weekly payments are paid to the family to help to support every child after the first.

1946   National Insurance for all working people. Everyone of working age has to contribute towards buying a stamp each week. Payments of money are paid to everyone when they are off work because of illness, when they are unemployed and when they are too old to work.

1946   National Health Service founded to provide free medical treatment for everyone.

Main achievements in science

1900–14   Development of electric light bulbs.

1900–14   Development of early cars; for example, the Rolls Royce Silver Ghost in 1906.

1909   First crossing of the English Channel by aeroplane.

1919   First crossing of the Atlantic Ocean by aeroplane.

1920s   Silent films.

1922   The B.B.C. began to broadcast.

1936   First daily programmes of television put out by the B.B.C.

1940   Radar warning system developed to spot enemy aircraft.

1945   Atom bombs dropped on Japan to end the war in the Pacific.

1946   Atomic research stations established in Britain.

1946   Increasing replacement of steam engines by electric and diesel engines on the railways.

1949   First jet airliner.

1960   Russians launch the first man into space.

1969   Americans landed on the Moon.

Index